ISBN 978-0-243-20251-5
PIBN 10565089

1 MONTH OF
FREE
READING

at

www.ForgottenBooks.com

By purchasing this book you are eligible for one month membership to ForgottenBooks.com, giving you unlimited access to our entire collection of over 700,000 titles via our web site and mobile apps.

To claim your free month visit:

www.forgottenbooks.com/free565089

English
Français
Deutsche
Italiano
Español
Português

www.forgottenbooks.com

Mythology Photography **Fiction**
Fishing Christianity **Art** Cooking
Essays Buddhism Freemasonry
Medicine **Biology** Music **Ancient**
Egypt Evolution Carpentry Physics
Dance Geology **Mathematics** Fitness
Shakespeare **Folklore** Yoga Marketing
Confidence Immortality Biographies
Poetry **Psychology** Witchcraft
Electronics Chemistry History **Law**
Accounting **Philosophy** Anthropology
Alchemy Drama Quantum Mechanics
Atheism Sexual Health **Ancient History**
Entrepreneurship Languages Sport
Paleontology Needlework Islam
Metaphysics Investment Archaeology
Parenting Statistics Criminology
Motivational

Treasurer's Account.

RECEIPTS AND EXPENDITURES FOR THE YEAR 1889; ENDING MARCH 1, 1890.

STATE AND COUNTY TAXES.

Paid Solon A. Carter, State Treasurer............ $830 00
Alonzo T. Pinkham, County Treasurer........ 831 89

SCHOOLS.

Paid Charles W. Hayes, Treasurer of School Board $628 29
For City of Dover Hayes & Hills proportion,.   19 43
                                                 ———
                                              $647 72

——— —

Paid Martin V. B. Felker, 1st selectman,...	25 00
John C. Hanson, 2d selectman'.............	25 00
William P. Jenkins, 3d...................	25 00
Albert Varney, collector....................	30 00
Charles W. Hayes, treasurer,..............	15 00
Edward L. Young, town clerk..............	16 00
Wm. S. Hayes, school board..............	15 00
Edwin L. Jenkins, school board......	15 00
Charles W. Hayes, school board......	15 00
Edwin L. Jenkins, supervisor............,........	3 00
George D. Nute, supervisor.............	
Charles L. Huckins, supervisor...............	3 00

$187 00

——— —

SUPPORT OF POOR.

——— —

Paid Ira A. Locke, for support of John H. and Ellen M. Church, from Feb. 4, 1889 to Feb. 4, 1890, 52 weeks, at $2.50 per week............	$130 00
Isaac G. Felker, for support of Nath'l Church from Feb. 4, 1889, to Feb. 4, 1890, 52 weeks, at $1.00 per week.................	52 00
J. Frank Seavey & Co., 1 suit of clothes for J. H. Church........,.......··.............	8 00
J. Frank Seavey & Co., 2 shirts for J. H. Church.....................................	2 00
J. Frank Seavey & Co., 2 pair hose for J. H. Church	1 10

Paid J. Frank Seavey, & Co , 2 pairs overalls for
J. H. Church 1 30

J. Frank Seavey,&Co.,mittens for J.H. Church,   50

Thomas H. Dearborn & Co., 16 yards cotton for
Ellen M. Church...........................   1 12

Thomas H. Dearborn & Co , 5 yards of ging-
ham for Ellen M. Church..................   35

Thomas H. Dearborn & Co., 2 pair hose for Ellen M. Church.............................   76

Thomas H. Dearborn & Co., 2 vests and 2 pair
pants for Ellen M. Church.................   2 00

George A. Reynolds, 1 pair boots for J. H.
Church 2 50

George A. Reynolds, 1 pair boots, E. M.
Church....................................   1 50

Dr. M. B. Sullivan, for medical attendance on
Mrs. John Cole...........................   85 00

Hayes & Hodgdon for merchandise delivered
Augustus A. Davis, from Dec. 17. 1889, to
Feb. 4, 1890, 7 weeks at $2.00 per week......   14 00

$302 13

DAMAGE BY DOGS, 1888, PAID 1889.

Paid Ezra E. Demerritt, 5 sheep killed........... $14 00

Ivory H. Kelley, 2 sheep killed by dogs......   6 00

Fred L. Richardson, 1 sheep killed by dogs...   3 00

Wm. C. Twombly, heirs of, 2 turkeys........   3 00

$26 00

DAMAGE BY DOGS, 1883, PAID 1889, IN PART.

	Total damage.	Paid.
Paid Albert Varney, 21 sheep	$81 00	$10 44
John H. Kelley, 5 sheep......	17 50	2 26
Oliver K. Hayes, 1 sheep.....	3 50	45
George O. Hayes, 1 sheep.....	3 50	45
James J. Griffin, 2 sheep......	8 00	1 03
George Berry, 1 lamb	3 00	38
Charles W. Hayes, 1 sheep....	3 50	45
Alonzo D. Nute, 1 sheep......	3 50	45
Joseph Fernald, 1 sheep......	3 50	45
F. L. Richardson, 1 sheep.....	4 00	52
Henry Swallow, 1 sheep.......	3 50	45
Alfred Demerritt, 2 sheep.....	7 00	90
C. R. Cocking, 1 sheep.......	4 00	52
Abagail Demeritt, 2 sheep....	7 00	90
W. S. Hayes, 2 sheep........	7 00	90
August Biederman, 1 sheep....	3 50	45
		$21 00

ROADS AND BRIDGES.

Paid A. T. Coleman, 3384 feet plank and timber...	$59 22
Demeritt & Burnham 2750 feet plank at $18 per M....................................	49 50
Hannah Rollins, 867 feet pine timber,........	8 68
Ezra E. Demeritt, 785 feet oak timber at $8.00	6 28

Paid John B. Huckins, 460 feet pine timber 4 60
Charles L. Huckins, 1328 feet pine timber 13 28
John C. Hanson, 705 feet timber for bridges
and glass for town house 11 78
Ira T. Jenkins, railing and spikes for Gerrish
bridge 4 84
John C. Hanson, labor on roads and bridges... 33 27
Frank W. Sanders, labor on road 3 35
Wm. J. Sanders, labor on road 2 00
Isaac G. Felker, 2 1-2 days work with team .. 6 15
Charles H. Gerrish, labor on Gerrish Culvert .. 1 50
Wm. P. Jenkins, 290 1-2 hours labor on culverts 43 57
James L. Paul, 13 1-2 hours labor on road 2 02
Josiah R. Mitchell, 33 hours labor on road 4 95
Samuel Emerson, 10 days work and use of der-
rick 28 00
M. V. B. Felker, 18 1-2 days work on roads
and bridges 27 75
Ellery M. Felker, 38 hours work on C. bridge .. 5 70
"   "   1 day's work on road mach.. 2 00
"   "   30 hours work on road 4 50
J. B. Huckins, 2 days work on C. Bridge 3 00
C. L. Huckins, 2 3-4 days work on C. bridge . 4 13
Ivory H. Kelley, 10 days on roads and bridges. 15 00
David B. Hayes 18 1-2 hours work on road... 2 77
Charles R. Cocking, 119 hours work on road.. 17 84
Wm S. Hayes 4 1-2 days work on C. bridge... 6 37
"   "   200 feet plank............... 3 60
Ira B. Hill, labor on road 8 75
Albert Weeden, 1 day's work on road.... ... 1 50
John W. Emery, 36 loads gravel 5 40
Wm. H. H. Twombly, 127 feet plank 2 29
John W. Hall, 2 1-2 days work on C. bridge .. 3 75
                                               _____
                                               $397 34

Paid Wm. P. Jenkins 89 hours breaking roads, 1889			$13 34
" " 18 1-2 " " 1890			2 77
Edwin L. Jenkins, 81 " " "			12 15
Samuel D. Glass, 86 1-2 " " "			12 97
Charles R. Cocking 41 2-3 " " "			6 25
Frank P. Morrison, 12 1-2 " " "			1 86
John C. Hanson, 35 ' " "			5 31
Fred L. Richardson 7 3 " " "			10 95
C. W. Hayes, 10 " "			1 50
Albert Varney, 86 1-2 " " "			12 97
Martin V. B. Felker, 55 2-3 " " "			8 33
Frank W. Sanders, 48 1-2 " " "			7 29

$95 69

MISCELLANEOUS BILLS.

Paid E. B. Lane for books, check-lists and stationery	$ 7 00
Dr. John R. Ham, for reporting births and deaths...	1 00
J. H. Seavey, for iron spikes and wire.......	11 75
Beach Soap Co., for loss of time and damage to Co., April, 1889.............................	30 00
Scales & Quimby for printing town report for 1888...................................	13 75
Frank M. Jeffs, for loss of time and injuries received April 11, 1889, on road.............	88 50
John B. Huckins, for taking affidavit of Augustus A. Davis................................	1 00
Frank P. Morrison, for board and services rendered Frank M. Jeffs.....................	25 00
John C. Hanson, for time settling with Jeffs..	4 00
Wm. P. Jenkins, for " " "	2 25
Dr. G. B. Emerson, medical attendance on F. M. Jeffs..................................	28 50

Paid Dover Sewer Pipe Co., 77 feet, 8 inch pipe.... 16 27
Geo. M. Church, for keeping public watering
place for 1889................................ 3 00
M. *N*. B. Felker, expenses to Concord to settle
with state treasurer............................. 5 30
M. V. B. Felker, 2 1-2 days to settle with Jeffs 5 00
"   "   postage and spikes........ 72
"   "   settling Davis family........- 3 00
"   "   1 day settling with commis'rs 2 00
John C. Hanson for 2 feet wood for town house 1 25

$249 29

TREASURER, IN ACCOUNT WITH TOWN OF MADBURY.   DR.

To cash in treasury March 1, 1889.............. $916 19
State, county, town and school taxes collected.. 1155 76
Dog tax collected............................. 46 00
Highway tax collected......................... 31 16
Savings bank tax.............................. 1252 27
Railroad tax.................................. 110 38
Literary fund................................. 37 31
Literary fund interest in C. W. Hayes' hands... 11 40
County for support of county paupers.......... 302 13
John C. Hanson, rent of town house........... 2 00
Henry L. Felker, collector 1886, in full........ 69
"   "   "   1887, " 2 07
Albert Varney,   "   1888, in part....... 85 18

$3952 54

TREASURER, IN ACCOUNT WITH TOWN OF MADBURY,   CR.

Paid state tax $830 00

Paid County tax...................... .... 831 89
    Schools 647 72
    Salaries of town officers.:................ ...... 187 00
    Support of poor............................... 302 13
    Damage by dogs, 1888, paid 1889........... 26 00
        "   " 1883, "   " 21 00
    Roads and bridges............. .... 397 34
    Breaking roads............................. 95 69
    Miscellaneous bills.......................... 249 29
    Auditors 2 00
    Balance in treasury March 1, 1890........... 362 48

$3952 54

CHARLES W. HAYES, Treasurer.
MARTIN V. B. FELKER, Selectmen
J. C. HANSON,   of
WM. R. JENKINS,   Madbury.

We, the undersigned, certify that we have . examined the foregoing accounts and find them correctly cast and properly vouched, and the balance in the treasury correctly counted.

IVORY H. KELLEY,   Auditors.
THOMAS W. FERNALD,

Madbury, March 1, 1890.

STATEMENT OF THE FINANCIAL CONDITION OF THE TOWN, MARCH 1, 1890.

State, county, town and school taxes assessed 1889 $1252 75
Highway tax assessed 1889........................ 521 95
Dog tax assessed 1889............................ 47 00

Total assessment for 1889.................... $1821 70

DUE THE TOWN.

Outstanding, Albert Varney's list, 1888 .... $20 41
     "   "   "   " 1889 .... 96 03

$116 44

Cash in the treasury March 1, 1890 .... 362 48

$478 92

DUE FROM THE TOWN.

Damage by dogs, 1889, payable March 1, 1890.

Ann Cole, 1 sheep killed $3 00
Ivory H. Kelley, 2 sheep killed 6 00
George O. Hayes, 1 sheep killed 3 00
Ezra E. Demeritt, 2 sheep killed 6 00

$18 00

The balance of the damage $9.99, done by dogs 1883
     payable March 1, 1890 .... 9 99

$27 99

ABATEMENTS, 1889.

Augustus A. Davis on poll and dog $1 48
Ira L. Eddison "   " 48

$1 96

ABATEMENTS, 1888.

Augustus A. Davis on real estate and poll........ $3 98
Daniel W. Shannon on poll....................   85
Charles Parks on poll....   85

    $5 68

ABATEMENTS, 1887.

Charles Woodus, on poll......................   47
Augustus A. Davis, Jr., on poll............-.....   47

    94

ABATEMENTS, 1886.

Ed. Taylor, on poll..........................   05

Total abatements made in 1889........ .... $8 63

SCHOOL MONEY FOR 1889.

Raised by law.... .... $581 00
Literary fund................................   37 31
Literary fund interest........................   11 40
Dog tax.....................................   18 01

    $647 72

MARRIAGES.

Married at Dover, Jan. 1, 1889, by Rev. H. F. Wood, Frank W. Sanders, aged 25, white, farmer, 1st marriage, born at Madbury, son of W. J. Sanders, born at Alexandria, farmer, and Harriet E. Sanders, born at Madbury, house-wife and Carrie A. Burke of Alton, aged 22, white, school teacher, 1st marriage, born at Wolfboro, daughter of Samuel S. Burke and Mary J. Burke, born at Portland, Me.

Married at Dover, May 7, 1889, by Rev. H. F. Wood, Isaac G. Felker, aged 63, white, widowed, farmer, born at Barrington, son of John Felker, born at Barrington, farmer, and Mehitable Felker, born at Barnstead, housewife, and Margaret A. Hamblin of Newton, Mass., widowed, aged 51, housekeeper, born at Charlestown, Mass., daughter of Thomas Larabee and Phebe Larabee.

Married at Durham, by Rev. S. H. Barnum, Fred E. Locke, aged 28, white, 1st marriage, farmer, born at Madbury, son of Ira A. Locke, born at Dover, farmer, and Lydia V. Locke, born at Madbury, housewife, and Mary A. Amerzeen of Durham, aged 23, spinster, 1st marriage, born at Portsmouth, daughter of Wm. H. Amerzeen, born at Newcastle, and Mary A. Amerzeen, born at Lewiston, Me.

BIRTHS.

Born at Madbury, July 14, Lydia S., a female, living, white, 2d child of George M. Church and Martha J. Briggs, white, carpenter, born at Dover and Alexandria, aged 36 and 31, born at Madbury, Aug. 18, a male, living, white, 2d child of Arthur L. Simpson and Lydia E. Hill, farmer, born at England and Madbury, aged 30 and 36.

Born at Madbury, Sept. 4, Ralph R., a male, living, white, 4th child of Reuben Swallow and Elizabeth, white, mill hand, born at England and Dover, aged 34 and 31.

DEATHS.

Died at Madbury, Jan. 26, Mary V. Felker, aged 74, born at Milton, female, white, married, housewife, daughter of Wm. Mathes and Sarah Varney, born at Lee and Milton, disease, general debility, report by D. T. P. Chamberlain, M. D., Dover.

Died at Madbury, Feb. 20, Mary F. Hill, aged 69 years, 9 months, 15 days, born at Durham, female, white, married, housewife, daughter of Odiorne, disease bronchitis, report by John R. Ham, M. D., of Dover.

Died at Madbury, Sept. 11, Sarah E. Gerrish, aged 42 years, 1 month, 24 days, born at Madbury, female, white, single, housework, daughter of Samuel C. Gerrish and Catharine Elliott, born at Durham and Pittsfield, disease diarrhœa, report by L. H. Green, M. D., of Newmarket.

Died at Madbury, Nov. 6, John Cronin, aged 4 months, 12 days, born at Lee, male, white, single, son of Wm. Cronin and Kate Lynch, born at Portsmouth and Charleston, Mass., disease, canker and dropsy of the brain, report by L. G. Hill. M. D., of Dover.

Died at Madbury, Feb., James J. Griffin, not reported.

FINANCIAL REPORT OF SCHOOL BOARD FOR 1889, ENDING MARCH
1, 1890.

RECEIPTS.

Balance in treasury March 1, 1889................ $78 92
Balance in treasury, District No. 2, March 1, 1889.   11 31
Received of town treasurer, school money for 1889. 628 29

$718 52

EXPENDITURES.

No. 2.

Paid Mrs. Laura E. Morrison for teaching 21 weeks
     spring & fall terms, at $6.00 per week......... $126 00
     Mrs. Laura E. Morrison, for teaching 9 weeks
     winter term, at $6. 50......................   58 50
     Edward Pendexter, for 1 cord pine wood......   3 00
     E. L. Jenkins, for 1 stove door frame........   1 25
        "   "   " 1 box chalk.............   20
        "   "   " 1 broom.................   30
        "   "   " sawing 1 cord pine wood...   50

$189 75

No. 3.

Paid Miss Annie Hall, for teaching 20 weeks spring
     and fall term, at $6.00 per week............. $120 00

Paid Miss Annie Hall, for teaching 9 4-5 weeks winter term, at $6.50 per week.................... 63 70

C. W. Hayes for 2 cords pine wood.......... 6 00

"   "   2 boxes chalk at 14 cents.... 28

W. S. Caldwell, 1 cord oak wood............. 5 00

C. W. Hayes, for cash paid Cate for work on chimney 75

"   "   cash paid Mrs. G. Mendom for washing school buildings........ 2 25

"   "   brick for chimney.............. ·90

"   "   2 keys for desk................. 25

"   "   fitting 3 1-2 cords wood........ 1 75

$200 88

No. 4.

Paid Miss Georgia E. Twombly, for teaching 20 weeks spring and fall terms at $6 00 per week. $120 00

Miss Lura M. Sleeper, for teaching 10 weeks winter term at $6.50 per week.............. 65 00

Wm. S. Hayes, for 2 days whitewashing and cleaning school house........ 2 00

"   2 locks for shed............ 1 05

"   paid A. I. Hall for lumber.... 1 40

"   paid J. D. Young, one sill ... 1 00

"   paid Wm. H. Buzzell, for planing, etc................ 75

"   paid J. H. Seavey, for nails.. 55

"   paid Littlefield & Co., for 3 stove legs.................. 75

"   one day with horse.......... 2 50

"   "   paid J. Twombly for 4 1-2 days work on shed.......... 11 25

Wm. S. Hayes, 1 box crayon............,.... . 15
" " 1 broom.................... 35
" paid John Lucas, 10 feet hard
wood...................... 6 00
" paid George Berry, 10 feet
mixed wood................ 6 00
" fitting wood............... 1 25
___ ___
$220 00
E. L. Jenkins, tuition of Herbert Swallow to
March 9, 1888............................. 12 85
E. L. Jenkins, tuition of Mattie Emery and
Herbert Swallow three terms to Jan. 10, 1890. 29 98
___ ___
$42 83

TREASURER OF SCHOOL BOARD. DR.

To balance March 1, 1889, for the year 1888...... $78 92
" " 1, Old District, No. 2.......... 11 31
School money for 1889........................... 628 29
___ ___
$718 52

TREASURER OF SCHOOL BOARD CR.

By school No 2.............................. $189 75
" " 3............................... 200 88
" " 4............................... 220 00
Tuition....................................... 42 83

Balance Town School District..............$53.75

Balance School District No. 2.............. 11.31   65 06

                                             ————

                                           $718 52

CHARLES W. HAYES, Treasurer.

WM. S. HAYES,   ⎞
E. L. JENKINS,   ⎬ School Board.
CHARLES W. HAYES,   ⎠

We, the undersigned, have examined the foregoing accounts of the school treasurer, and find them correctly cast
and properly vouched.

IVORY H. KELLEY,   ⎞ Auditors.
THOMAS W. FERNALD,   ⎠

Due the school district of Madbury from the school
    district of Durham and I. Blake Hill, for tuition
    of Harry and Frank Hill, 30 weeks each at 49
    cents per week each....................... $ 29 40
From District No. 1, balance of school money
    not legally expended, about................ 225 00

SCHOOL REPORTS.

CENTRAL SCHOOL.

The three terms of the school year were taught by Mrs. Laura E. Morrison.

ROLL OF PERFECT ATTENDANCE.

Spring term—Sallie A. Berry, May R. Berry, Alice L. Demeritt, Frank H. Hill.

Fall term—Florence E. Biederman, Florence Kelley, Florence Pendexter.

Winter term—Grace L Richardson, Annie L. Richardson, George A. Brown.

	Spring.	Fall.	Winter.
Length ot term	10	11	9
Teachers' wages per week	$6 00	$6 00	$6 50
Whole No. of different pupils	26	28	26
Average daily attendance	23	25	20
Percentage of attendance	.9583	.9259	.9090
No. of Pupils not absent	4	8	3
" " in reading	26	28	26
" " in spelling	26	28	26
" " in penmanship	20	23	26
" " in arithmetic	21	21	24
" " in geography	12	10	12
" " in grammar	1	1	1
" " in book-keeping	1	2	2

One of the greatest hindrances to the advancement of this school is irregular attendance. Parents should endeavor to have their children in the school room every school day in the term, if possible. For without prompt attendance the scholar falls behind his or her class-mates, gets discouraged and so fails to receive the full benefit of the school. Another thing in regard to this school I think should be distinctly understood, that is that the school house is not to be made a place of idle resort by persons having no interest in the school.

Boys who do not consider their own interests enough to attend school, but choose rather to spend their time in idleness, are not likely to exert much influence for good in the school room, and I think it very imprudent for the teacher to encourage anything of this kind.

A few words in regard to dismissing school during school hours. Of course there are occasions when the teacher would be entirely justified in so doing. But it seems as though as the teacher is only required to be in the school room six hours a day, five days in the week, she should find ample time to attend to personal affairs without intruding upon school hours Regular hours, as well as prompt attendance, should be required.

E. L. JENKINS, Visiting Com.. Center School.

_____

SCHOOL NO. 3.

This school was taught the whole year by Miss Annie Hall of North Nottingham. Miss Hall had taught 12 terms and came here highly recommended, and I think I speak the minds of the whole school and district when I say she has maintained her high standing as a teacher throughout the entire year. Order and discipline superior, progress and thoroughness good.

Roll of perfect attendance—First term, Frank Caldwell, Willie T. Fernald, Frank W. Jones and Bertie Reynolds. Second term, Frank Caldwell, Willie T. Fernald.

	Spring.	Fall.	Winter.	Year.
Length of term.............	10	10	9 4-5	29 4-5
Teachers wages per week...	$6 00	$6 00	$6 50	
Whole No. of different pupils	11	10	13	16
Average daily attendance..	10	9	10	10
Percentage of attendance...	.9999	1.00	.909	
No. of pupils in reading....	11	10	13	16
" " in spelling...	11	10	13	16
" " in penmanship	5	5	5	6
" " in arithmetic.	8	8	12	13
" " in geography.	2	2	2	2
" " in grammar..	4	4	5	6
" " in history....	1		2	
" " in physiology.	1			1
" " in book keep'g	4	4	6	7
" " in algebra....	4	4	3	5
" " in phys. geog.	3	3		1
" " in rhetoric...				1

SCHOOL NO. 4.

Spring and summer terms of 10 weeks each were taught by Miss Georgia E. Twombly. Spring term commenced April 22, and ending June 28.

Number of pupils, 7 ; average daily attendance 6 ; percentage of daily attendance, .8555 ; No. of pupils in reading, 7 ; spelling, 7 ; penmanship, 7 ; arithmetic, 7 ; geography, 6 ; grammar, 1 ; history, 3 ; book-keeping, 1.

Summer term commenced September 9, and ending November 19. Number of pupils, 13; average daily attendance, 12; percentage of daily attendance, .9230; number of pupils in reading, 13; spelling, 13; penman-hip, 13; arithmetic, 13; geography, 9; grammar, 3; history 4.

Roll of honor—Fred W. Bennett.

Miss Twombly has taught this school five terms and was offered the winter term, but declined. As a teacher she is one of the best.

Winter term of 10 weeks was taught by Miss Lura M. Sleeper, commencing December 9, and ending February 21. Number of pupils, 13; average daily attendance, 11; percentage of daily attendance, .8462; number in reading, 13; spelling, 13; penmanship, 13; arithmetic, 10; geography, 8; grammar, 4; history, 7; book-keeping, 1.

Roll of honor—Minnie C. Hayes.

Miss Sleeper is a teacher of 23 terms experience. Order, progress and thoroughness was good, especially explanations. This term as heretofore was a success.

GENERAL REMARKS.

We live in an age of progress, of change. Our "history is not a mere succession of events connected by chronology; it is a chain of causes and events," and in our country the education of the nation is the chief cause that determines its destiny. "The boy is the father of the man and the children of today are the society of tomorrow. We see in our infant sons the coming voters, and in our girls the mothers of the next generation of sovereign citizens, and that policy that governs our schools will presently control the government of the nation." Every parent is bound in duty to remember that his child and his neighbor's child is going forth into human society capable of being a blessing or a curse, and that he has before him at the end of his earthly career, a hereafter. It is the parents duty to see that his child receives such training as shall fit him to be a benefactor to his race, by having in his mind and heart the spirit and character of his Divine Master. The petty jealousies and differences that will always arise in human society, should never be allowed to interfere with the high interests of education and truth. While I would guard our schools with jealous care against clashing doctrines and sectarian controversies, I believe that "there are certain great religious truths which are admitted and believed by all christians. All believe in the existence of a God, the immortality of the soul, and the responsibility in another world for our conduct in this," and the great principle of right and wrong. Let us all, on this common ground unite to impress deeply on the minds of our youth the great principles of sobriety, industry and frugality, chastity, moderation and temperance, and all those other virtues which are the ornament of human society and the basis on which our republican institutions are founded.

WM. S. HAYES,
E. L. JENKINS,   } School Board.
CHARLES W. HAYES,

CPSIA information can be obtained
at www.ICGtesting.com
Printed in the USA
BVHW040255231118
533509BV00031BB/4261/P